life giver

a 4-week Bible study

by lara williams

www.LaraWilliams.org

© 2015 lara williams
all rights reserved

Printed by Create Space
© Copyright 2015 Lara Williams

All Rights Reserved

ISBN 978-1-5085-1330-8

Unless otherwise noted, Scripture quotations are from the Holy Bible, English Standard Version, copyright © 2001, 2008, 2011 by Crossway.

Printed in the United States of America

table of contents

about the author………4

introduction………5

week 1 :: let God define me………8

week 2 :: intercede………23

week 3 :: forgive………39

week 4 :: encourage………55

conclusion………71

about the author

Lara Williams has experienced the beauty of freedom in Christ and desires to lead other women into a powerful walk of faith with their Lord. As a speaker and author, Lara has a way of candidly sharing her real-life struggles with a touch of humor, while leading the listener into places of deep theological truths -- truths meant to affect our Mondays and Tuesdays.

Lara has also authored *To Walk or Stay* and *Then Came Jesus*, and co-authored a number of Bible studies available at QuenchBible.com. You can connect with Lara online and find out more about her resources at LaraWilliams.org.

speaking :: http://larawilliams.org/speaking
blog :: http://ToOverflowing.com
facebook :: http://www.facebook.com/lara.g.williams
instagram :: http://instagram.com/laragwilliams
email :: laragwilliams@gmail.com

introduction

This Bible study grew from a lesson I taught to a MOPS group — which, for the record, is a group of ladies that I absolutely love because I *get* moms of preschoolers. I get that your clothes have perpetual food stains because your child has mentally concluded that your leg is a napkin, and that you don't wear white jeans for that very reason, and that you can't identify that smell in your minivan. I get that. I still live in that land. *But I digress.*

So I spoke to that sweet group of ladies about embracing our identity in Christ as women, regardless of our circumstance. And as I prepared for that talk, God showed me that embracing who we are in Christ not only profoundly affects us personally — stirring up hope and peace and joy regardless of our situation. But believing what God says about us has profound effects upon our relationships with others.

Did you catch that? Let me repeat it just in case you skimmed that last paragraph like I'm tempted to do when I read introductions:

> [Believing what God says about us has profound effects upon our relationships with others.]

That's when it came to me. We can either be "life suckers" or "life givers" in our relationships.

You know you want to say "life sucker." Go ahead.

A life sucker sucks the life out of a relationship because she often gives into her own insecurities. With her attitude and actions, she all-but-begs for affirmation. She needs life to go as *she* has planned and people to do what *she* expects in order to have even an *ounce* of temporary soul-rest. And when people or circumstances fail her, she spirals into hopelessness.

Nobody likes being or being *with* a life sucker.

But then there's the life giver. Her eyes stay focused upon God -- not perfectly but consistently. She recites God's declarations over her and His promises to her. She wrestles her heart into places of faith, learning to trust Him even when she can't see the outcome because she knows Who's in control. She stands secure on the character of her God and the identity He declares over her. Therefore she's so full of love and grace that she can't help but spill Him out onto those around her. She pours life into her relationships because she's so full of God.

We all like being and being *with* life givers.

I've been (and can still be, if I'm not on-guard) a life sucker — depending on people or circumstance to give me the abundance my soul craves. And it isn't pretty. It always leaves me restless. But when God graces me with the ability to be a life giver because I walk secure in what He says about me, I experience the freedom to live and love the way He intends. And there's truly nothing like it.

> For freedom Christ has set us free;
> stand firm therefore, and
> do not submit again to a yoke of slavery.
> Galatians 5:1

We're going to spend the next four weeks looking at four necessary aspects to being a life giver in our relationships. And because we have so much that tries to steal life from us, I want these four lessons to be easy to remember. Which is why I created an acronym with the word " L I F E. " *Because good teachers create acronyms, right?*

> Let God define me.
>
> Intercede.
>
> Forgive.
>
> Encourage.

You will also notice this box at the end of each day:

Use this space to write down the "one thing" you want to meditate upon throughout that day. It may be a prayer. It may be a promise you read from His Word. It may be something God says about you as His child. Just note the one thing that He presses most heavily upon you that particular day.

Finally, know that I've prayed for you. I've asked God to graciously use this short walk through His Word to draw you closer to Himself. I've prayed that He would root you even deeper into the identity He declares over us in Christ. I've prayed, knowing that His love for you and me goes further and wider than anything we can humanly grasp.

May we walk fully and freely in the abundant life our Father gives in Christ, that we would be empowered to give life to others.

The first necessary step to being a life giver is to come into a relationship with God through Christ. If you have not yet taken that step of faith -- believing that Jesus died in place of the punishment due to you and me and that He rose and that He will come again -- then today can be the start of that relationship. Seek out a trusted pastor or friend to walk with you into this new journey.

week 1
let God define me

day 1

I would encourage you to start each daily lesson with prayer.

> Lord, I want to see You, know You,
> love You, and honor You.
> Reveal Yourself to me through my time in Your Word.

This week we'll look at the vital shift that needs to take place in order for us to be life givers in our relationships. The shift? Let God define me.

Remember, a life sucker sucks the life from relationships. She's so needy for people and circumstance to define her, that she drains people dry. She subconsciously asks over and over and over and over again, "Do you think I'm pretty? Do you think I'm smart? Do you think I'm a good mom/wife/daughter/friend?" And relationships become heavy with expectation, stripped of any joy, and driven by insecurities.

What questions are you tempted to subconsciously ask of others in your search for identity? In what areas have you wrestled with insecurity?

We've all been there, living out of insecurities. We dress a certain way in efforts to hear affirmation from other humans. We criticize out of desperation to build ourselves up. We manipulate because the thought of losing seeming control sends us into a panic. We need someone — anyone! — to say or do certain things in order for us to sense some peace or hope. *All characteristics of a life sucker.*

But people are only human, just like us. They will fail to sufficiently answer our identity questions or meet our expectations because they're naturally self-focused. *Just like us.* So living our days dependent upon other volatile, emotional, short-sighted humans to define us will always leave us thirsty, because they weren't created to quench our thirst.

Read Psalm 63:1-8 aloud. *Yes, out-loud. I believe there's great power in physically hearing the Word of God.*

Read the text again noting what it reveals about us as humans.

The text reveals that humans long for a "satisfaction". Humans have thirsty souls

Read the text one last time noting what this text reveals about our God.

The text reveals that God is the only answer to the human's need for satisfaction. Only God can provide the true fulfillment to our needs, that humans seek. His lovingkindness is greater than life.

How are these truths about God meant to impact you, especially in relation to your places of insecurity?

Do not look in worldly people/places for "satisfaction". God can eleminate insecurities because he is the only one who can truly love you, accept you, guide you, etc. God is the only one who can satisfy your thirsty soul. Live to only need satisfaction from God.

What or who have you been tempted to "drink of" in efforts to find a quenching for your soul-thirst?

Trying to be the best of the best is something that has given me "satisfaction", because when you're the best "no one can look down on you". Although, God is the best of the best and acceptance & love from him is all you really need.

♥ <u>God alone gives the soul-satisfaction that we so desperately crave.</u> No person and no thing can ever perfectly fill the void. This broken world will always leave us thirsty for more.

So what does the text tell us to "do" in order for us to find soul satisfaction in Him?
(look for the two verbs in v. 6)

<u>Meditate</u> on thee. Look to him for soul satisfaction.

How will that look in our daily living?

Praising God with joyful lips.
Lifting up our hands in thy name.
Eliminating the thirst for worldly satisfaction
 & receiving it from God, the only one who
   can fill the void.
He alone quenches our thirst.

Close out your time today in prayer with the Lord. Confess those places of insecurity you noted above and ask Him to speak truth into those specific areas of your heart. Ask Him to give you a deeper understanding this week of His view of you in Christ.

> my soul thirsts for you,
>
> my flesh faints for you,
>
> as in a dry and weary land
>
> where there is no water.
>
> Psalm 63:1

my one thing: Psalm 63:7
"Because thou hast been my help, therefore in the shadow of thy wings I will rejoice."
- also -

"God alone gives the soul-satisfaction"

day 2

Start today with a prayer.

> Speak Lord, we're listening.

Jesus came to quench our soul-thirst. He came to satisfy our longing to be seen and known and heard and redeemed. He came to give us a new name, a new identity, firm in Him.

Yet too often we fall into the rut of looking to others to define us. We linger on what they say about us. We're tempted to look at ourselves through their opinions and their criticisms and their praises. And in the end we're left wanting because the opinions of people fluctuate.

Read John 12:42-43 aloud.

Why did the authorities not speak of their faith in Jesus?

They did not speak of their faith in Jesus because the Pharisees would put them out of the synagogue.

What did the authorities love most?

They loved the praise of men more than the praise of God.

How do you see this same mentality affect our identity issues? Why do you think we as humans crave the approval of other humans?

It is easy to think that if people do not accept you then they will "put you out" (defriend) you.
We as humans want to be accepted & liked by others. No one wants to feel like an outcast or not part of a crowd/group.

Waiting around and seeking after the approval and praise of others is flat-out tiring. It's time consuming and mentally draining. But it's tempting because people are tangible. Their words are audible. Their affirmation is physical. Whereas choosing to meditate upon and believe what God says about us takes effort. It takes conscious choice. But the reward is priceless. The result is freedom.

Read 2 Corinthians 5:17-21 aloud.

Read the text again noting what Paul says about our identity in Christ.

a new creature
old things are passed away
all things are new

Read the text one final time noting what the text reveals about our God.

He did not put their tresspasses unto them.
He gave his only begotten son
So that we might be made the righteousness of God in him.

In Christ, how much does God approve of us? What can we do to gain even more approval?

We can reconcile his word
God approves of us so much that he has given us the ministry of reconciliation.

Those last two were trick questions. Because of what Christ has done, we are fully approved of by the Father through faith. We can't do or say anything to change His gracious approval. God's desire and plan for us is that we walk our days secure in what He says about us, regardless of what enters our today.

To pour life into our earthly relationships rather than suck them dry, means we begin here — face-to-face with our Maker. We begin by knowing who we are, which flows from knowing WHOSE we are. We let *Him* define us rather than scrounging for affirmation from other needy humans. If we don't, we'll never find the satisfaction we crave.

> The water that I will give (her) will become
> in (her) a spring of water welling up to eternal life.
> John 4:14

Close out your time in prayer. Ask God to show you ways in which you seek the approval of man more than Him. Then ask Him to continue to make His truths alive in you. Ask Him to set your feet firm in your identity in Christ regardless of what people may say or do.

my one thing: Let God define us rather than needy humans. Know WHOSE you are!

day 3

Open your time today with a moment of prayer. Confess any places of struggle and ask for Him to guide you with wisdom through your time in His Word.

We need You, Lord. Always. And forever.

I know how messy I am. I see my weaknesses and failures. I see how quick I can overreact to my kids or how natural it is to think something rude about those I'm called to love. So one reason I personally struggle to believe what God says about me is because I *know* me too well.

Do you ever struggle to believe what God says about you? Why?

But His view of and declarations over me and you do not depend upon what we do or don't do. God's declarations over us rest solely and securely in what Christ has already done. Our identity in Christ remains firm because God initiated relationship with us and sustains us through His immeasurable grace.

Read Ephesians 1:3-10 aloud.

Read the text again noting the adjectives Paul uses to describe our new, secure identity in Christ.

According to this text, why did God restore us to Himself?

> Blessed be the God and Father
>
> of our Lord Jesus Christ...
>
> Ephesians 1:3

I recently became overwhelmed with this Ephesians text. As I read it again and again, it finally became clear to me that Paul is absolutely *taken* with God's gracious pursuit of us fallen humans. He can't get passed the humbling grace of God that calls us sons and daughters in spite of our many failures. In fact the entire first three chapters of Ephesians is Paul's beautiful overflow of gratitude to this amazing God.

God set us apart, not because of how good a mom we can be or how great a friend we can be or how amazing a teacher/wife/sister/Christian we can be. He set us apart to be holy purely by grace. Purely through faith. Purely out of *His* goodness. It's truly scandalous.

Read Ephesians 2:10-22 aloud.

Read that text again noting how Paul describes us before coming to Christ.

What does the text teach us about our identity *in* Christ?

Read the text one last time noting what it teaches us about God.

How are the truths in this text meant to change our response to life circumstances?

Close your time in prayer. Thank the Lord for the identity He declares over you. And then pray He would guide your thoughts back to truth today when circumstance and emotion tempts you to believe otherwise.

my one thing:

day 4

Open your time by writing a prayer in the space provided.

> Lord, I thank You that You are:
>
> I praise You for Your grace as seen through:
>
> I confess that:
>
> I ask You to show me Yourself today.

There are two key avenues to allowing God to define us.

One, we read what He says about us. That's what we've been doing all week -- gleaning truths from His Word. And that's exactly what we want to keep doing every single day. Because life gets crazy and can tempt us to believe lies about our God and lies about ourselves in Christ. So we have stay in the Word. *Have to.*

But two, we need to stay in constant conversation with Him, especially when we're tempted to doubt. *Constant. Conversation.* We have to bring every thought captive to truth, otherwise we will live being swayed to and fro by this world.

It sounds simplistic, but our hearts are deceptive. If we don't stay on-guard, we quickly fall into the trap of looking to people or circumstance to give us our purpose and meaning for life. Yet God alone never changes. His declarations over us never fade. He alone can be trusted.

Read Jeremiah 17:5-8 aloud.

What does Jeremiah teach us about "trust" in this text? (see vv. 5 and 7)

Why do you think our hearts are tempted to trust in what *people* say about us and do for us?

Practically speaking, in day-to-day living, what can we do to actively trust what God says so that we will be like that deeply rooted tree?

I don't want to be a dried up shrub, trying to suck life from every one around me. I want to be a woman who stands secure by the river of my God, drinking the water He gives. A woman confident in my Daddy's declarations.

By grace, through faith in Christ, God says, "My precious child, you are righteous, beloved, accepted, forgiven, and free. My beautiful daughter, you are pure, lovely, set-apart, and always on My mind. Before you lived a single day, I embroidered you."

Yet our hearts deceive. Life happens, people say and do things, and our hearts are tempted to doubt. Let me give you some examples. *Hypothetically*, your child yells from behind a slammed door "YOU'RE THE MEANEST MOMMY IN THE WORLD!" or your boss insists "You'll never amount to anything." In those moments we have choice. In Christ we can take all the emotion that those types of situations bring straight to our God rather than blindly letting the words of others define us.

We ask for His insight, "Am I the meanest mommy or the laziest employee or the worst wife? Is there something I need to confess -- something You want to change in me?" We want to know if God desires to shed needful things from our lives.

But after a time of soul-searching confession before the Lord, it's vital that we turn our hearts to *His* declarations, "What do you say about me?" We then wash our hearts with the water of His Truth. We choose to believe what *He* says rather than live swayed to and fro by other equally needy humans.

That may mean (definitely will mean) we run to the laundry room, shut the door, and preach a mini-sermon to our heart. But in the end, allowing Him to define us positions us to be life-givers.

Read Galatians 4:3-7 aloud.

Read the text again noting what God says about our identity in Christ.

What does it mean that you are an heir of God? What are the benefits to being a son or daughter of God?

How is that title of "heir" meant to affect you when people say hurtful things or when life gets painful?

By faith in Christ God looks at us and says "my son" or "my daughter". No one can steal that relationship. Nothing can hinder His love in our lives. And that reality is meant to change how we move through our days.

Close your time today with prayer, thanking Him for what He said to you today from His Word.

my one thing:

day 5

Start today with praise. Praise God for who He is and what He says about you in Christ. Then ask Him to graciously speak to you today.

I praise You, Lord, for You are...

I want us to close out this week looking at a very intimate passage. But before we go further, it's vital that I make something clear.

Until we come to Christ by faith -- meaning that we believe He died for our individual sins, took the judgment we deserve, rose from the dead, ascended to the Father, and will come again one day -- until we believe that gospel message, we're considered an "enemy" of God. That means that we *all* stand before this holy God condemned until we believe that Christ took the punishment we deserve.*

I say that because we're going to look at an Old Testament text today, meaning that it was written before Christ came to this earth. However, if you and I are in Christ -- heirs of the Father -- the things God says in this Psalm absolutely apply to us as adopted children of God. So read and be encouraged.

Read Psalm 139 aloud.

Read it again noting what the text says about us as humans.

Read the text one final time noting what the text reveals about our God.

How does this text encourage you?

Which specific truths from this text could you choose to meditate upon even when others reject or betray or speak unkind things to you?

We cannot flee from His presence. We cannot run from His sight. Our days are numbered. Our hair is counted. Our lives are in His hands.

God's promises to us and declarations over us trump anything that anyone else may say. If we're going to be life givers, regardless of what life brings, we must begin here. We begin by bringing our thoughts captive to what *He* says. We let *Him* define us.

Close out your time in prayer, thanking Him for the gracious identity He declares.

* If you have never trusted Jesus as your personal Savior, please seek out someone with whom you can learn more about this life-changing decision. Life with God is an adventure that can't be compared to anything else.

my one thing:

discuss or reflect upon week 1

1 :: What area(s) of life challenge you most when it comes to believing what God says about you, i.e. motherhood, employment, marital situation? Why?

2 :: Of the adjectives God uses to describe your identity in Christ, which ones mean the most to you right now in your life? Why?

3 :: Practically speaking, in day-to-day living, what can you do to bring your thoughts captive to your true identity in the Lord? How can you stay diligent to let God define you regardless?

4 :: Discuss *one* of the "my one things" that God impressed upon you this week.

week 2
intercede

day 1

Begin by asking God to reveal Himself even more intimately this week, especially regarding our calling to intercede.

> Show me Yourself, Lord God,
> as well as the power and necessity of prayer.

Last week we talked about step one to being a life giver in our relationships: *let God define me*. And that step is absolutely crucial. In fact, if we don't begin there and camp out there, allowing God to define us, we will easily slip into life sucker mode — depending on people and circumstance to give us the hope and peace and joy we crave. And that mode never works. *Ever. I've tried.*

The goal is to be at the place where people and circumstance no longer hold the *power* over our soul stance. Yes, hard things happen. Devastating things at times. Yes, people hurt us. And yes, feelings and more feelings come. And God is so tender to our humanity. He's patient with our process. But in Christ we don't have to *live* or *remain* in the place of unrest. We may visit for a while but we don't have to take up residence.

It takes a pressing into Him, especially when we're tempted to doubt what He says *about* us and what He promises *over* us. But when we fill our hearts with His truths, continually communing with Him when feelings flare, we're positioned to be life givers, even to those who try to suck the life from us. *Can I get a witness?*

So we begin by allowing God to define us. Step two to being a life giver: intercede.

Did you catch the "I"? Intercede? L-I-F-E? So clever, huh.

Intercession or prayer is simply talking with the God of the universe. *A simply unbelievable gift.* It's communing with Him. And He tells us to intercede or pray continually. As in, all the time.

It's not that *He* needs us to pray. He's God. It's that *we* need to pray. *We* need His continual perspective. We're the ones whose hearts deceive. And through our communing and resulting intercession, He graciously calls forth His will into our livesb and onto this earth.

He's the only One who sees the beginning from the end. He's the only One who can strengthen us from the inside out. He's the only One who can guard our hearts with the peace that passes all human understanding. He's the only One who can give Divine wisdom and perspective. And He graces us with the privilege of prayer.

Prayer is a privilege given to us in grace.

So let's spend some time today looking at the aspects of prayer.

Read Psalm 100 aloud.

Now read it again listing *how* the Psalmist tells us to enter the presence of God.

According to this Psalm, whom are we to focus upon when we enter His presence? Us or God?

Read Philippians 4:6-7 aloud.

Read the text again noting how we are to combat the anxious places of our heart?

How do you typically battle against anxiety?

What are the benefits/results to combatting anxiety in the way this text instructs?

It isn't that God needs us to pray. *We* need us to pray. We constantly need a shift in perspective from our short-sighted, self-focused vision to His eternally perfect, omniscient vantage point. And when we do, His peace guards us. His peace rests upon us because we rest in the character and promises of our King.

Close out your time today praying as these texts instruct. Sing to Him. Praise His name for Who He is. Thank Him for His faithfulness. *Then* present your requests to Him. Combat any places of angst with the method Paul describes in this Philippians text.

Depending on the severity of the situation causing your heart trouble, you will most likely have to keep coming back into God's presence throughout the day. But He promises that when we do, He will faithfully guard our hearts with a peace that passes human understanding.

my one thing:

day 2

Ask God to continue to reveal the things taking up residence in your heart that steal the peace filled, abundant life Christ died to give you.

I need Your vision, Lord.

Yesterday we looked at different aspects of prayer -- praise, thanksgiving, presenting requests. Today we will begin looking at when and for whom we're to pray.

Prayer for ourselves

Praying for ourselves goes hand-in-hand with last week's theme of "letting God define us". We as humans naturally, internally respond to life circumstances and to the people involved in those circumstances. It's what we do. But our hearts aren't reliable. Our hearts typically *don't* lead us to the right action or right conclusion.

Read Jeremiah 17:9-10 aloud.

What does this text tell us about our heart?

Who perfectly knows and sees our heart?

When circumstances challenge our soul-rest, we desperately need to seek after our God in prayer. When people hurt or disappoint us, we desperately need to seek after our God in prayer. When our kid or boss or spouse or parent or neighbor steps all over our soul, we desperately need to seek after our God in prayer. Before we speak or take action, the wise choice is to begin with intercession for our own perspective and our own soul, asking Him to align our heart with His truth.

In fact, we see this type of prayer throughout the Psalms.

Read Psalm 43 aloud.

Now read the text again looking at the Psalmist's emotional state. Compare his emotional state when he focuses upon his enemy vs. when he focuses upon his God.

How did he transition to a place of hope? What did he do? What led him there? (v. 3)

Describe a time when prayer changed your perspective from despair to hope.

The Psalmist had been hurt. Probably betrayed. Probably near killed. And he felt a lot of things. He felt oppressed by God. He felt vengeful towards his enemies. He felt angry and depressed. *All understandable.* And God didn't condemn him for those feelings. *Just as God doesn't condemn us for our feelings.*

Feelings are normal. They're a thermometer. They reflect our human response to life. But they aren't always reliable. Following where they lead often means destruction. So when feelings flare, the place of blessing is at the feet of God. We need to wash our emotions with the truth of His character. We need to intercede for our own souls, openly and honestly. It isn't until after we gain *His* perspective that we can wisely respond to the circumstances of life.

Close out your time asking God to reveal any emotions that need His healing touch. Preach truth to those places in your soul that cry out in despair. Remind your heart of true things -- aspects of our God that stir hope even in desperate situation. He remains the same yesterday, today, and forever.

> Hope in God; for I shall again praise Him,
> my salvation and my God.
> Psalm 43:5b

my one thing:

day 3

Complete the following sentence for your opening prayer:

> Reveal my heart, Lord.
> Give me perspective regarding…

Yesterday we talked about praying first for ourselves when our emotions flare due to changing circumstances and the actions of others. Today we're going to take that one step further by looking at how we can respond *specifically* when someone criticizes our character. Because if there's ever a time for personal intercession, it's when we feel attacked.

Personally, this one has tripped me up more times than I'd like to admit. Instead of responding humbly to the criticisms that another may offer, my natural inclination is to get proudly defensive and point my finger with a "Oh yeah. Well you…" But I've realized something. Defensiveness interrupts my fellowship with God. Defensiveness insists that *I* defend my character rather than trusting in my Father to stand in my defense. It insists that I've got life all figured out.

> Defensiveness interrupts my fellowship with God.

The truth is that we don't have it all figured out. And not only that, we live in a fallen world with an enemy who continually attempts to destroy the witness of God's children. So we *will* be criticized and insulted. The question is, how will we respond.

Read Matthew 5:11-12 aloud.

Read the text again noting whom Jesus calls "blessed".

Why do you think he would call the "reviled" or "insulted" blessed?

That word "reviled," or "insulted" as some translations say, means to "defame, chide, or taunt". So our Lord calls us blessed when, on account of walking by faith in God, we're taunted by others. I'm sorry but that's completely twisted. That goes directly against my natural tendencies. But the truth is that when we die to self and walk secure in what *He* says of us, the taunts and criticisms of others no longer determine our peace or lack thereof.

Read 1 Peter 2:21-25 aloud.

What example did Jesus leave for us to follow?

How did He combat against the reviling from others? (v. 23)

What would that kind of response look like in your own life?

How does His example make you *feel*?

There are two possible reasons for the criticisms of others. Either the accusations are true or they're false. Either way, we have choice in our response. We can defend ourselves or we can respond like Jesus responded. We can entrust ourselves to the just One. And that "entrusting" comes through intimate, continual intercession.

But let's be honest. When our character is attacked and our feelings flare, we need something tangible, something practical that we can fall back on with regard to our words. Otherwise, it can get ugly.

So regardless of *how* someone may point out our inconsistencies or failures or their *perception* of our failures, the most life-giving response we can give in that moment is "Thank you for telling me. I'm going to pray about that." Say it with me, *out-loud*...

Thank you for telling me.

I'm going to pray about that.

After we respond with that phrase, we then actually pray. We intercede for ourselves. We ask God for His opinion of our heart. We seek His perspective. We remain open to the possibility that He wants to use this to change us to look even more like Jesus. *It's called humility.*

Often it isn't until after we've prayed for ourselves that we're able to rightly see. It isn't until after the emotion has settled that we're able to humbly respond.

Life isn't about being right. It's about love. It's about Jesus. It's about leaving a mark on this planet that points others to the One their soul craves. And responding to the criticisms and taunts of others with humble intercession stops quarrels and spurs true change -- both in us and in our relationships.

Close out your time today asking God to give you the strength to say that "thank you" phrase the next time you are criticized. If someone has recently attacked your character, spend some time praying for perspective. Maybe they saw something you don't see, or maybe they simply spoke out of their own insecurities, either way intercession proves vital to being a life giver in that relationship.

my one thing:

day 4

Open your time with prayer, specifically regarding wisdom for any strained relationship in your life.

> Father, my relationship with ... is strained.
> Grace me with Your wisdom.

The past two days we've talked about praying first for ourselves when circumstances get wild or people get rough. And that's absolutely necessary if we want to be life givers. But this next step is also essential if we're going to pour out life into our relationships.

Praying for others

As long as we live on this planet, people will hurt or disappoint us because they have their flesh to deal with, *just like we do*. They will say things and do things that break our spirit, *just like we will*. But in those moments we have a choice to make. We can allow what others say and do to define us, or we can take the emotion that life brings to the God of the universe and intercede.

If there's anything that comes natural to us as humans, it's to fixate upon and criticize the weaknesses in others. In fact, we as humans seem to have an uncanny ability to identify all the things that need to change in others, while downplaying or completely missing all the mess that clutters up our own heart. I think they call that self-righteousness. *Blah.*

I wrote about this in my book *To Walk or Stay* because when my husband and I went through our darkest times, it was easy for me to point fingers and blame him. But God tenderly and lovingly revealed my own messed-up heart. He showed me that I wasted so much time criticizing Adam rather than interceding for him. And as his helpmate and sister-in-Christ, intercession was, *and continues to be*, my call. In fact, prayer is our calling even towards our enemies!

Read Matthew 5:43-45 aloud.

Read the text again noting what Jesus tells us to do for our enemies.

What reasoning does He give for these instructions?

> I say to you, love your enemies
>
> and pray for those who persecute you.
>
> Matthew 5:44

Now read Luke 6:27-36 aloud.

Read the text again noting what Jesus tells us to do for our enemies.

What reasoning does He give for these instructions?

Given our natural bent towards retaliation and criticism, practically speaking, how can we respond in love to those who "persecute" us?

Give a personal example of a time when, by God's grace, you responded in love. Or give an example of a time you didn't respond in love and what God taught you through that experience.

I can't do it. When left to me I want to retaliate and bite back. I want to defend myself and insist that God smote those who hurt or betray me. And Jesus knows that. Our Father is tender to our pain. But He also knows the place of freedom for our souls.

Jesus said these things so we could rightly see our heart in light of the unconditional love of our God. He wants us to see our desperation for His empowering. He wants us to run to Him for strength. And He wants us to know that His grace abounds when we fail. We can't love and pray for those who hurt us apart from Him. Yet in His mercy He stands ready to love others *through* us, even our enemies, by way of intercession.

Close out your time today in prayer. Ask God to reveal your heart meditations, specifically regarding those who are more difficult for you to love.

my one thing:

day 5

Ask God to grace you with wisdom to know what you could pray for specifically regarding your most difficult relationship.

I'm listening, Lord.

We're going to close out our week talking a bit more about praying for others, even when they hurt or disappoint us.

Praying for others

I mentioned it yesterday, but we as humans have this natural ability to identify weaknesses in others. And often times when we see inconsistencies or sin or weaknesses in others, we're prone to criticize. We *may* criticize verbally. And a barrage of verbal criticism can definitely destroy relational intimacy. But I've realized that the *internal* criticisms become even more disastrous to our relationships.

Personally, I can bite my tongue while having a world of unrighteous judgments in my heart. Just because I don't say a thing doesn't mean I've made a God-honoring choice. What honors my God and brings blessing to my own soul is when I turn even the *internal* criticisms into intercession.

I have the choice to turn internal criticisms into intercession.

We can do this as a wife, mom, daughter, friend, sister, roommate, employee. The list is endless. When we stand firm in who God says we are, we're positioned to be life givers through intercession. And believe me, the results from intercession immeasurably outweigh the results from critical defensiveness.

So what can we pray for others? Let's see what Scripture teaches.

Read Ephesians 1:15-23 aloud.

Read the text again noting what Paul specifically prays for the Ephesian believers.

Now read Ephesians 3:14-21 aloud.

Read the text again noting what Paul prays in this text.

Now comes the more difficult work. I want you to think of your most strained relationship -- the one in which you find it most challenging to be a life giver. Ask God to forgive you for any critical spirit you've harbored towards that person -- confess that unlove as sin. Then in the space below, using similar phrases to the Ephesians' texts, write out a prayer for that person. Intercede for their weaknesses rather than criticize.

As long as we live on this planet people will always disappoint or hurt us. Just like we will disappoint or hurt them. Because we all have our flesh to reckon with. But you and I have a choice. In Christ, we don't have to live bound to a critical spirit -- sucking life from our relationships. We can choose to be life givers by turning criticisms into prayer.

Close out your time by asking God to grace you with His vision for those around you -- *especially those you find most difficult to love.* Then stand in the gap for the heart struggles that they face. I promise, it's a way better choice. It's the life-giving choice.

my one thing:

For practical encouragement
in your personal prayer life,
visit www.MillionPrayingWomen.com

discuss or reflect upon week 2

1 :: How has this week's lessons challenged or changed your view on prayer?

2 :: Why is continual intercession important?

3 :: Practically speaking, what can we do in our daily lives to help us further incorporate continual intercession?

4 :: Discuss *one* of the "my one things" that God impressed upon you this week.

week 3
forgive

day 1

Start today with prayer.

> Lord, show me the great grace I'm under
> that I would give great grace to others.

There's only one place to begin when it comes to forgiving those who hurt or wrong us. We have to begin with a robust view of the great grace and forgiveness under which we stand in Christ. Otherwise, judgment makes more sense.

If we've put our trust in Christ, in essence we declare, "I can't do it. I can't live up to God's beautiful, holy perfection. So I put my trust in the One that God sent to *be* my perfection. I trust that because of Jesus, the Father sees me as righteous."

We can't live up to the righteous standard of our holy God. And He knows that. The entire Old Testament is evidence that we as fallen, selfish humans are not able. But God, being rich in grace, had a plan. He sent Jesus to *be* our righteousness. He sent Jesus to live the perfect life so that we don't have to. He sent Jesus to take the consequences we deserve so that *we* could be made right with Him. It's called radical grace.

Read Ephesians 2:1-10 aloud.

Read the text again noting the description of us before we enter into the grace of God.

Read the text again noting Paul's description of God.

Read the text one last time noting the description of salvation.

What do these truths do to your own spirit? How does this text give perspective to your own relationships?

You and I stand before God by grace alone. None of us deserve to be in His holy presence. *None of us*. Yet because of His great love, He made a way. And we enter that way by grace and through faith alone. No amount of works makes us righteous enough. No amount of money makes us acceptable enough. No amount of sacrifice makes us lovely enough. We come to Him purely and solely by grace. He calls us righteous simply because we believe in the Righteous One.

Those are *shoutin'* words. To think that we stand secure before a holy God because of Christ, in spite of our many many many failures, should cause our knees to hit the ground in praise. It's an awesome gift.

But something can happen inside of us when someone hurts or fails *us*. For some reason we as humans can get momentary amnesia as to the great grace that blankets our lives. Before the dust has time to settle we're standing with the proverbial gavel in hand ready to declare our offenders "Guilty as charged. Now pay up." We forget how much we've been forgiven.

Read Matthew 18:21-35 aloud.

Summarize the parable in a few short sentences.

How is this parable meant to affect our relationships? Is there any offense not covered by God's (and in turn our) forgiveness?

Share about a time when you experienced undeserved forgiveness from someone. And/or share about a time when, by God's grace, you forgave the "undeserving" offender.

Grace as seen in forgiveness has nothing to do with the offender. Grace as seen in forgiveness has everything to do with the decision of the giver, *regardless* of the other.

You and I don't deserve the grace God shows us through the death and resurrection of Christ. We don't deserve it. We can't earn it. Our gracious God freely gives it *in spite of* our continual failures. Once we enter in and truly grasp His pursuit of our selfish, rebellious heart, the only natural response is to pour out the same grace onto those who sin against *us*. It's that radical kindness that will lead others to repentance.

Close out your time in prayer. Ask God to give you an even wider view of His grace so that you will be ready to pour out that same grace upon others when they offend you. Because as long as we live on this planet, people will hurt and offend us, *just like we will them*.

my one thing:

day 2

Open up your time in prayer, asking God to reveal any places of unforgiveness in your spirit.

Open my eyes, Lord.
Show me any unforgiveness I've harbored.

As long as we live on this planet, we will rub shoulders and share space with other fallen humans. Humans, *just like us*, who are prone to selfishness. And when we live among naturally selfish beings, we're susceptible to the hurt or disappointment or betrayal found in relationships. It's the nature of earth. *It's why Jesus came.*

But admit it. It's easy to fall into the trap of entitlement. It's easy to hold our expectations with rigidity, defending a stance that cries out "I have a right to (fill in the blank)". It's natural to demand retribution and impose the law onto those who offend. But that stance is rooted in pride. That stance will inevitably bind up our soul with bitterness, because people will fail. *Just like we will fail.* And when people fall, *we* have a choice: freedom or bondage.

Read Ephesians 4:30-32 aloud.

Read the text again noting below what our actions can do to the Holy Spirit.

How do we "grieve" the Holy Spirit? (v. 31)

What does it look like in our lives when His Spirit is "grieved" within us?

When we come to faith in Christ, the Bible teaches that His Spirit seals us. That's a mark of permanence. We are His Temple -- the Spirit's dwelling place. However, every single day, every single minute, we have the choice to be *filled* by His Spirit. And His *filling* can be seen in our lives. His *filling* empowers us to be life givers, regardless of the other person.

Read Galatians 5:16-26 aloud.

Read the text again noting what it looks like when we are filled with, and responding out of, our flesh.

Now read the text one last time noting what the "fruit" of being filled by His Spirit will look like in our lives.

When someone hurts us, how can we "stir Him up" so that we are filled with His Spirit in our response?

Being filled by His Spirit is a choice we get to make, even when someone hurts or disappoints us. But we have to be purposeful. For me it looks like escaping to a quiet place (a.k.a. the bathroom) and preaching truth to my spirit. I pray. I recite Scripture. I pray some more. I may turn up some praise songs or listen to a sermon. But regardless of the "how", I fill my mind and heart with truth. I begin with Him rather than chasing after the inevitable feelings. And I ask for His perspective. Only then am I equipped to be a life giver.

I've responded, and still respond, in both ways. I've had relational wounds that have sent me into deep soul rebellion. Times when I chose to live with harbored unforgiveness, grieving His Spirit within. But I've also had relational wounds to which I responded, by God's grace, *out of* the great grace that covers me. As an act of the will, I chose to speak forgiveness. And the result was, and will forever be, freedom.

> But God, being rich in mercy,
> because of the great love with which he loved us,
> even when we were dead in our trespasses,
> made us alive together with Christ...
> Ephesians 2:4-5

Unforgiveness on any level grieves God's Spirit within us. It steals life from us. It feeds our flesh demands. It causes bitter roots to dig deep. *And the enemy loves that.* But regardless of the offenses against us, God wants to set us free from unforgiveness.

Depending on the degree of pain an offense caused to your soul, you may think that forgiveness is impossible. But Christ came to empower us to do the flesh-opposing, seemingly impossible things. By His grace, we can forgive.

Close your time in prayer asking God to show you anything that hinders the filling of His Spirit in your life, specifically regarding unforgiveness.

my one thing:

day 3

Open your time by asking God to reveal any bitterness that has taken root in your soul. His plan for us is freedom.

> Lord, uncover the things in my heart
> that steal life from me.

Unforgiveness left to dwell in our soul eventually turns into bitterness. And bitterness has a high price. Bitterness stems from pride and demands retribution. It insists a debt be paid. And it steals the joy and peace Christ died to give. It causes us to knowingly and unknowingly speak curse over others. Which always and forever ends in bondage and cursing for *us*.

Read Ruth 1:19-21 aloud.

After devastating tragedy in her life, Naomi asked to be called "Mara" which means "bitter". **Read the text again noting how bitterness had affected Naomi's perspective. Whom did she blame?**

How and/or what did bitterness steal from her? What does bitterness steal from us?

Naomi had been through much tragedy. Her emotions were both normal and justified. *And God is so tender to our emotions.* But when we harbor a spirit of blame, as Naomi did, bitterness results. Bitterness births when we feel as if we deserve better and someone needs to pay. Yet when we allow bitterness towards others, *or towards God*, to take up residence in our souls, we will lose the joy He intends. The joy that comes from trusting our God to be faithful and good and love.

The only solution to bitterness is trust -- trusting God to be who He says He is. Trusting that He is sovereign and faithful. When we preach that sermon of trust to our soul, bitterness dissipates.

Bitterness can't remain in the same space as faith. Truly believing that God has us where He wants us with purpose stirs up rest for our spirit. We rest in knowing that His allowances into the lives of His children come directly from His omniscient, omnipotent, loving, Father hands. We rest in knowing that His allowances will be *ultimately* for our good and His glory. And when we rest there, bitterness bows down.

Read Matthew 10:28-31 aloud.

Read the text again noting *why* Jesus instructs us not to fear. What does He tell us about the character of God?

How could this aspect of His character confront the bitterness in our spirit?

How do you think fear is related to bitterness?

I know that I know that some of you have been through horrific trials. And we don't always know why God allows what He allows -- the betrayals and the sufferings and the offenses. But when we begin with Him and His character -- that He's sovereign over the birds of the air and sovereign over my life as His child -- bitterness has no place.

> He who dwells in the shelter of the Most High
> will abide in the shadow of the Almighty.
> I will say to the Lord, "My refuge and my fortress,
> my God, in whom I trust."
> Psalm 91:1-2

Bitterness ultimately says, "I am closing myself off to the possibility that God wants to use even this, *even this*, for my good and His glory." Bitterness stands as a proud guard around our hearts. It demands answers and it's fueled by fear.

God has used the painful, relational hurts to teach me a very important lesson. He has used the offenses to teach me that *He* is enough. That *He* is sufficient. That *He* is sovereign. And when I stand secure in His character, bitterness has no place. It has no right to keep me in bondage. It's only when we confront the bitterness in our soul with the truth of God's sovereignty that we'll find the freedom that comes with forgiveness.

Close out your time in prayer. Preach the sermon of trust to any bitter places in your soul. Declare your faith in the God who both sees and knows your trials, and Who promises to work all things together for your good.

day 4

Begin today by asking God to further unveil any harbored unforgiveness in your spirit. Ask Him to make you *ready* to forgive, come what may.

> Open my eyes to any lies that I have believed.
> Make me ready to forgive any offense that may come.

As I've thought more about unforgiveness, I've realized that unforgiveness often stems from a "rights" mentality. "I have a right to her respect." Or, "You have a right to him treating you well." *Rights*. We base all of our expectations upon seeming rights. Rights tell us what we deserve. They tell us what we can demand. They tell us when we can hold a grudge. They even promise us the peace we crave. But what if I told you that "rights" lie.

When we stand upon our rights, demanding certain things from others in order to have soul-satisfaction, we enter into the territory of *conditional* love. When we expect others to do something for us before we will do something for them, we forfeit the grace of Christ -- just like that parable of the ungrateful servant.

What "rights" have you been tempted to stand upon in your relationships?

The truth is, as humans, we really only have one right. We have a right to God's judgment. We have a right to God's wrath. We're the rebels standing before a perfect, holy God. Yet He moves *towards* us. He pursues us in love. He takes the punishment we deserve and places it on His righteous Son in order that we would be set free from our sinful, selfish rebellion. It's truly scandalous.

Read Isaiah 53:3-6 aloud.

Read the text again noting the words that describe what was laid upon Christ.

Jesus took that for you. He took that for me. The beautiful One came down to this planet and took the wrath we deserve so that we could be set free. You and I have no "rights". We live solely under grace.

Yet we can still slip into the mindset that we *deserve* something from others. We can still become deceived by the fleshly lies that whisper of our rights. So we have to stay on guard. If we want to live our lives pouring out life and grace onto those around us, then we have to take our thoughts captive to truth, moment-by-moment. We have to keep our minds set on the grace under which we stand.

Read 2 Corinthians 10:3-6 aloud.

Read the text again and note how Paul describes the weapons we've been given in Christ. (v. 4)

What can these weapons empower us to do with our minds?

To what weapons do you think Paul is referring?

In Christ we have three key weapons that empower us to take our thoughts captive to truth. One is His Spirit -- whom we talked about earlier this week. The second is His Word -- which we've dug into throughout this study. And the third is prayer -- communing with the God of the universe.

These three weapons work together to empower us to take our thoughts captive to truth so that when someone offends us, we don't have to move into "rights" mode demanding our way. It may look something like this:

You find out that your dearest friend has talked negatively about you behind your back. Or even more debilitating to the soul, your spouse has been inappropriately texting another woman. *Or worse*. The natural thing is to demand rights. "I have a right to her loyalty. I've been her friend for fourteen years and I would never talk about her behind her back like that." Or "I have a right to his fidelity. I'm his wife. He promised to cherish me."

Those are all correct thoughts in a sense. Yes, in a perfect world, we would hope that friends would give us loyalty. And yes, in a perfect world, fidelity honors both God and our spouse. But we don't live in a perfect world. And the truth is that people fall. So how can we take our thoughts captive when we've been offended? We employ the weapons we've been given.

We pray. We pray truth. We pray truth to stir up the empowering of His Spirit so that we can respond with love and grace. "Lord, I need You. I'm hurt. I'm angry. I'm confused. So I need Your perspective. You promise to be my refuge. You promise to work all things together for the good of those who love You. You promise to guide my steps as I seek after You. I know that You have allowed this for reasons I may never fully understand. So I trust You, Lord. Minister healing to my soul. Mend these wounds. Give me the words to say. And teach me what You would have me learn."

Depending on the level of anger or betrayal, we may have to commune with Him loudly and multiple times...*per hour*. But we've been given mighty weapons to bring our thoughts captive to truth. In Christ, we don't have to respond to the offenses of others from the proud stance of our rights. We can seek after Him, allow Him to minister to our own souls, then respond in a way that will bring the most good.

We don't have any rights when it comes to our relationships with other fallen humans. Because humans fail. And standing on rights proves to be shaky ground. But in Christ we have a right to His empowering. We have a right to the weapons He promises. We have a right to peace when we seek after Him. We have a right to freedom. We have a right to receive and pour out grace simply because of Jesus.

Close out your time today asking God to reveal any "rights" you've harbored in your spirit when it comes to your earthly relationships. Spend some time in prayer laying down those rights. Depending on how deeply those rights bury into your soul, laying them down may take time. But the release of rights brings the freedom we desperately crave.

day 5

Ask God to teach you *how* to forgive, regardless of feelings.

> I believe that forgiveness is freedom.
> Lord, help me to forgive, regardless.

At this point we can probably all agree that forgiveness is best. Forgiveness, even of those who wrong us deeply, proves to be freedom for *us*. But there's one little thing that often gets in the way: our feelings.

Share about a time when your feelings have tried to get in the way of you forgiving someone who hurt you.

I'm a girl. And let me tell you. As a girl, I've got lots and lots of feelings. And I've got feelings about those feelings and feelings about those feelings. *Ad infinitum.* So when someone wrongs me, lots of feelings come to the surface and beg my attention. They typically insist on a good dose revenge and some loud conversations that include pointing fingers and a few "how dare you(s)" thrown in for added drama.

But the thing about feelings is that even though they are very very real. And often justified. They don't always lead us to the right action. *Remember what Jeremiah said about our hearts?* In fact I don't think my feelings have ever told me to forgive my enemies. *Ever.*

Yet Jesus commands forgiveness, for our good and His glory. And He means for it to be an act of our will, not necessarily an act of our emotions.

Read Colossians 3:12-17 aloud.

Read the text again noting how Paul describes us as Christ-followers.

Based upon that identity, what does Paul tell us that we can *choose* to "put on" if we are in Christ?

According to this text, what can we *do* to promote a forgiving spirit?

We have a choice. Regardless of our feelings, in Christ we have the choice to forgive even when we're desperately hurting. And that choice will bring soul-blessing.

Read Deuteronomy 30:19-20 aloud.

This text refers to the commandments that God gave the Israelites. And even though it doesn't specifically *talk* about forgiveness, **how can this text apply to us regarding forgiveness?**

God gives us boundaries and commands to protect us. He loves us -- perfectly and fully. He knows us -- perfectly and fully. And because He designed us, He knows what will lead us to our most blessed existence. When it comes to relationships, we will give life to others when we choose to forgive, regardless.

> Forgive each other;
> as the Lord has forgiven you,
> so you also must forgive.
> Colossians 3:13

How to Forgive

So the question becomes, "*How* do I forgive, especially when I'm hurting?" The answer? We turn to the One who forgives out of His amazing grace. We pray. We press hard into our Lord — the Forgiver of all sin. We seek refuge in Him and trust His covering. We meditate on what He says about forgiveness. We live authentic lives, allowing others to walk with us down the tearful road of releasing the debt we want another to pay. And then we believe God to do the heart-healing work that only He can do.

Feelings take time to line up with the willful forgiveness. But feelings eventually come. They *will* come. But until they do we command our soul towards obedience.

Forgiveness sets us free to love. It sets us free to give of ourselves without the need for others to do anything in return, because we've found fulness in our Lord. We see that everyone is the same — needy for a Healer and Redeemer. And when we see people through the lens of grace, unforgiveness has no place.

Close out this week's study with a time of honest conversation with the Lord. Confess any harbored unforgiveness. Tell God your honest feelings -- He already knows. Then speak truth over those feelings. Declare the verses we meditated upon this week regarding forgiveness. You may want to seek out a trusted friend to pray for you and with you as you walk the road of forgiving another. But however you get there, release others from a debt that's already been paid. Grace is the only road to becoming a life giver.

my one thing:

discuss or reflect upon week 3

1 :: How has bitterness ever stolen from you?

2 :: Share an example of a time when you chose to lay down your seeming "rights" in efforts to show grace.

3 :: Practically speaking, what can you do in efforts to forgive someone who offended you?

4 :: Discuss *one* of the "my one things" that God impressed upon you this week.

week 4
encourage

day 1

Open the week with prayer. Ask God to build even greater courage in you this week so that you would be equipped to impart courage to others.

> Teach me how to impart courage into others.

I know me. I know how God has gifted me — how He uniquely knit me together. I know how He has blessed me. But I also know that when left to my natural tendencies I'm selfish and short-sighted. I naturally think about "numero uno" and how things will affect *my* agenda. It's the plight of humankind.

That's why I need constant reminding of who I am in Jesus. That's why I run to the laundry room and shut the door and preach to myself. That's why I turn up some redeemed rap music to get my praise-dance on when things start turning south in la casa. *I'm not sure where all of this Spanish is coming from.* That's why I'm so thankful for friends who speak truth to me when lies try to push me around.

In your experience, what words or phrases give you courage to keep running this faith race when you are feeling low?

We all need courage at times to stand back up and keep moving forward by faith. So when I feel like dropping my sword and licking my wounds, I'm not going to call the person who will grovel in the pit with me. When I'm low I want to talk with someone who will help pick me up. Someone who will infuse life into my soul. Someone who will stir up the Spirit of God in me.

True encouragement — or the impartation of courage — doesn't come from building up someone's human ego. Because remember. We're weak and prone to wander. We can't see past the last minute and definitely can't control the outcome. So *true* encouragement doesn't come from self-elevation.

True encouragement arises when God's Spirit fills us full. When we lift our head because we remember Whose we are and what He promises.

Read Deuteronomy 1:29-31 aloud.

In this text, Moses is recounting the Israelites' past. He's reminding them of what he said when they were afraid to go into the "promised land". **Read the text again noting how Moses imparted courage to God's people. Of what *or Whom* did he remind them?**

How does this text challenge you?

I don't want someone to tell me how great I am. Well, that's a lie. I love it when someone tells me I'm great. But if I'm honest with myself, I see my discrepancies. I know my weaknesses. So I need reminding of my *God's* greatness. I need reminding of what *He* promises. I need *His* vision and *His* power stirred up within me.

> Why are you cast down, O my soul,
> and why are you in turmoil within me?
> Hope in God; for I shall again praise him,
> my salvation and my God.
> Psalm 43:5

If we're going to pour life into our relationships, we first have to know our God and know who we are in Him. Then we can empower others. We can stir up courage in others by reminding them of *true* things.

What are some truths regarding God's character and promises that prove foundational to His children walking forward by faith? These are words or phrases that you can keep in your "encouragement arsenal".

We all need courage to walk the roads God has for our today — some days more than others. And true courage arises when we remember what's true. Yes, there's a time to weep with those who weep. And I pray we would have wisdom to know when to keep silent. But there's also a time to remind. A time to stir up. To impart courage to take that next step by faith, eyes set on the One who sits enthroned outside the realm of time.

Close out your study today by asking God to let you see those who need courage. Then ask Him to use you to be the lifter of souls with words and prayers of truth.

day 2

Open your time in prayer asking God to reveal any fears or lies that may be hindering your courage to boldly walk forward by faith.

Lord, reveal what hinders my courage.

If there were ever a group of friends who were horribly handicapped at imparting true courage, it was Job's friends. Remember them? Job had been stripped of everything -- his material possessions were demolished, all of his children were killed, and he suffered from painful sores all over his body. We're talking the pit of discouragement. And then his friends show up on the scene.

Their best move came when they sat quiet and just wept with their friend. In fact they sat quiet with him for seven days and seven nights, until Job started the conversation. That's when they started fumbling in their impartation of courage. That's when they started making assumptions as to the "why" *behind* his sufferings.

Read Job 8:4-7 aloud.

Read the text again and then summarize what Job's friend said.

Job's friend was looking for an explanation. He was looking to explain the "why" behind all of Job's calamity. And he concluded that Job's sin and the sin of Job's children brought on this judgment from the Almighty God. Yet we see at the beginning of the book of Job that actually Job's *righteousness* brought on the suffering. It was *because* of his great faith that God allowed Satan to sift him.

Read Job 1:1 and 1:6-12 aloud.

Read the text again noting how God describes Job.

Who was in control of this situation, God or Satan?

What does this teach us about God's character and authority in relation to Satan's jurisdiction in our own lives as God's children?

Here's what can quickly discourage those walking through times of suffering. When we begin with circumstance and try to define God and His motives through the lens what we see, we often come to erroneous conclusions. And out of those erroneous conclusions we speak our short-sighted solutions. Discouragement can then follow. But when we begin with God -- declaring His character and promises without making quick assumptions regarding His motive -- we impart courage.

> I know that You can do all things,
> and that no purpose of Yours can be thwarted.
> Job 42:2

It wasn't until Job came face-to-face with the glory of God that his perspective changed. It wasn't until he and the others stopped trying to explain the "why" that Job's spirit lifted.

Read Job 42:1-6 aloud.

In vv. 3-4 Job restates what God just said to him in the previous chapters. Then Job responds to each statement in deep humility. **Read the text again noting what Job says about himself and his perspective now that he has seen God face-to-face.**

What does this text teach us about true courage? How will true courage arise?

All of us will fall into pits of discouragement at times. It's the nature of our fallen world and our limited perspective. But when we, or those we love, wrestle with discouragement, courage will arise *not* when we try to explain the why behind the suffering. Courage will arise when we turn our eyes onto the God reigning *over* the suffering. Courage will arise when we believe God to be the God that He's revealed Himself to be in the Scriptures.

Close out your time in prayer, asking God to free you from always needing to know "why". Then ask Him to put a filter over your heart and lips, that when courage is needed you would have the wisdom to speak truths regarding God's faithful character and steadfast promises.

my one thing:

day 3

Start your day with prayer, asking God to unveil any fear-based thinking in your spirit.

> You say, "fear not".
> Lord, help my unbelief.

Another hindrance that slips in and prevents us from being a life giver is fear. Ultimately fear reveals that our heart is focused upon someone or something other than God. We all do it. It's natural. Our human nature fears what we can't control or what we can't foresee. *But here's a little secret. You and I are not the ones in control. God is.*

When we're tied up in fear, we won't give life to others. We'll suck life from others in efforts to find some semblance of security. So when courage fades and fear rises, we need a good dose of truth.

Read Isaiah 41:8-10 aloud.

Granted, Isaiah was referring to the Israelites in this text. But if we are in Christ, then the Father adopts us as His own. Therefore the promises of His faithfulness remain. **Read the text again noting *why* we don't need to live in fear.**

When we're walking into unknown territory, tempted by fear, we need to know that we aren't alone. When we know that we know that someone goes before and behind us, fighting on our behalf, courage arises. And that "someone" is The Lord God Almighty!

Whatever you or I face, if we are God's child, we're never alone. He never leaves or forsakes us. He always goes before us and behind us. He always pursues us in love. He always fights for the throne of our heart.

Read Joshua 1:1-9 aloud.

Read the text again noting how many times God tells Joshua to be "strong and courageous".

Why **can Joshua be strong and courageous? What does God promise?**

How is God's Word connected to us walking forward with courage?

In what current situation is God calling you to be "strong and courageous"?

What aspects of God's character does He want you to remember, especially for the unknown roads He may call you, or a friend, to walk?

We aren't strong and courageous because we're big and bad. We can be strong and courageous because the Lord God is with us. He indwells us. He empowers us. When fear forces courage into hiding, we need reminding. Our friends need reminding. Our spouses and children and parents need reminding.

> Be strong and courageous.
> Do not be frightened, and do not be dismayed,
> for the Lord your God is with you
> wherever you go.
> Joshua 1:9

In Christ we don't have to live enslaved to fear. Yes, fear will come. It's a natural response to life's unknowns. But in Him we've been equipped by His Spirit and with the gift of His Word to walk forward with courage. We walk forward in strength, not because of us, but because of the One who goes before us in love.

That doesn't mean that fearful feelings won't come. They will. But remember, feelings may be real but they aren't always reliable. We take that next step by faith, often in spite of feelings, simply because we believe that God will remain faithful to His promises.

Close out your time in prayer asking God to reveal any fear that has recently gripped you. If we're going to be life givers -- givers of courage -- then courage has to first birth *in* us. Courage to take the next steps because of the One who goes with us.

my one thing:

day 4

Ask God to use you to encourage those that He has placed in your life.

Lord, give me eyes to see and words to speak.

Everyone loves to keep company with life givers. Because life givers bring life to our weary souls. Today we're going to look at a man who gave life through the gift of encouragement to those he encountered.

We meet up with him in the book of Acts.

Read Acts 4:32-37 aloud.

Read the text again and then briefly summarize the situation.

What was Joseph's nickname? What did it mean?

Can you imagine that kind of legacy? "Oh that's Lara. Around here we call her the daughter of encouragement." Talk about selfless and faithful.

Joseph, or Barnabas as he was called, served as a key character in Paul's first missionary journey. He became Paul's encouraging companion.

Read Acts 9:26-31 aloud. *The "he" that the text refers to is Saul, later known as Paul.*

Read the text again noting how the early apostles felt about Paul.

What did Barnabas do that could be seen as encouragement -- imparting courage into Paul and into the other apostles?

Paul had a reputation. The apostles feared because they knew that as a devout Jew Paul had Christ followers put to death. They didn't believe that Paul had truly become a disciple. But Barnabas believed. He testified to what he had seen in Paul. He stood up for the "new guy" even with the possibility of being ostracized. *Son of encouragement*. Then under the blessing of the apostles, he went with Paul on the first missionary journey to the Gentiles.

> (They returned) strengthening the souls of the disciples, encouraging them to continue in the faith...
> and saying that through many tribulations
> we must enter the kingdom of God.
> Acts 14:21-22

Later in Acts we see Barnabas stand up for the underdog again.

Read Acts 15:36-41 aloud.

Read the text again noting what Barnabas did to encourage Mark.

In light of Barnabas' actions, how do you think he would have defined encouragement?

How does his example challenge or encourage you?

People all around us, all the time, need courage to take the next step on the road God has for them to walk. And just think, God may want to use *us* to speak life and truth into their spirit. He may want to use *our* words to stir courage in another.

Close out your time asking God to empower you to leave a legacy of encouragement. Ask Him to show you the people around you who need a word of courage today. And then believe Him to give you the words to speak and the wisdom to know when to speak them.

day 5

Start today by asking God to deepen your fellowship with other believers.

Thank you, Lord, for the gift of togetherness.

There's one piece of the life giver puzzle that we've assumed throughout our time together. One necessity if we're going to *give* life. A backdrop to this entire study: *We have to be in relationship with others.* It sounds like a "duh" factor. But authentic fellowship can too easily be neglected.

In our self-focused, independent, "I can do it alone" world, we have to be purposeful if we're going to live life in authentic fellowship. Because if we aren't living life in intimate relationship with others, we'll never see when they need courage for the road ahead. We won't know the fears they're wrestling or the doubts they're harboring. We have to purposefully nurture the friendships God brings, otherwise they will fade with time. *They will.*

God didn't create us to live independent lives. He designed with the intent of fellowship and togetherness. It's why mankind wasn't complete until God crafted Eve. It's why the human race wasn't "very good" until there were two.

Read Galatians 6:2 aloud.

What does Paul tell us to do?

To "bear" means to carry. **Practically speaking, how do we help carry the burdens of others?**

Truly carrying the burdens of others necessitates relationship. Truly carrying means more than a quick dollar out of the car window to the homeless guy on the corner. It means more than a check in the mail. Truly carrying means relationship. And Paul says that when we carry the burdens of others, we fulfill the law of Christ.

Read Romans 13:8-10 aloud.

Read the text again noting what this text says about love.

In light of this Romans text, rewrite Galatians 6:2 below with a fuller explanation of the "law of Christ".

I tell my kids that we only have one rule in our home: *Love*. We love up (meaning that we love God with all our heart, soul, mind, and strength). And we love out (meaning that we pour out His love onto one another).

Everything falls under the law of love. If someone in our home is hitting, pinching, grabbing, or hollering at the other, then that person is not following the law of love. That person is not in the place of blessing. That *un*love reveals a heart issue. And when we're not following the law of love, there are consequences -- not only consequences in our heart but consequences to our relationships with one another. *And consequences from mommy and daddy.*

There's only one law in Christ. And to fulfill that law of love we have to be in (messy, real, intimate, complicated) relationships with others. Only then will we get the chance to give life.

> Love one another with brotherly affection.
> Outdo one another in showing honor.
> Romans 12:10

My daddy used to always say, "If I have five close, true friends, I'm a rich man." The truth is, we can't be close and intimate with everyone we meet. We can't bear *everyone's* burdens. And God doesn't expect us to. But as His children, He will bring a few people into our lives with whom He intends for us to live authentic. People we're meant to love and be loved by. People to whom we're graced with the chance to give life.

Close out your time talking with the Lord about your relationships. Ask Him to show you how you can intentionally deepen your fellowship with others. Trust Him to empower you to give life to those He graciously places on your path.

my one thing:

discuss or reflect upon week 4

1 :: How has fear ever caused discouragement in your life?

2 :: What truths or verses or phrases stir up the greatest courage in you? Why?

3 :: Share a time when the encouragement from a friend truly empowered you to keep walking forward by faith. What did they say or do that most affected your spirit?

4 :: Discuss *one* of the "my one things" that God impressed upon you this week.

conclusion

Being a life giver in our relationships -- even the messiest relationships -- begins with allowing God to define us. Once we stand secure in what He says about us, we're free to pour life into others.

We're free to intercede rather than criticize, because we rest in knowing that we're not the ones in control. We're free to forgive, because we remember that we stand before a holy God under a banner of grace alone. And we're free to encourage, because we refuse to live life in bondage to fear.

> If possible, so far as it depends on you,
> live peaceably with all.
> Romans 12:18

As much as depends upon us, may we live peaceably with everyone He places in our path -- the good, bad, and the ridiculous. May we know who we are in Christ, secure in the identity He declares. May He empower us to be life givers, regardless.

Let God define me.

Intercede

Forgive

Encourage

Today, I'm choosing life.

Made in the USA
Lexington, KY
06 May 2017

Made in the USA
Lexington, KY
06 May 2017